PYTHON FOR BEGI

I0016137

A STEP-BY-STEP GUIDE ON HOW TO PROGRAM WITH PYTHON

MARK ALLEN

Table of Contents

Introduction

Python is a cross-platform programming language. It can be used on various systems including Windows, Unix, Mac **etc.** It also comes with numerous modules that are cross-platform. However, Python has maintained a uniform user interface. Python supports integration with different database management systems (DBMSs). This means that you can access your data from a database with Python. This book explores every aspect of Python programming language. It will help you in preparing a solid computer programming foundation and learning any other coding language will be easy to you.

This book can provide any programmer with some interesting and fun codes to learn from.

This book will help the already experienced programmer more, but a beginner can learn a lot from it too. You're sure to find lots of helpful information within these pages.

Chapter 1: What is Python?

Python is a programming/coding language. It's one of the programming languages that are interpreted rather than compiled. This means the Python Interpreter works or operates on Python programs to give the user the results. The Python Interpreter works in a line-by-line manner. With Python, one can do a lot. Python has been used for development of apps that span a wide of fields, from the most basic apps to the most complex ones. Python can be used for development of the basic desktop computer applications. It is also a good coding language for web development. Websites developed with Python are known for the level of security and protection they provide, making them safe and secure from hackers and other malicious users. Python is well applicable in the field of game development. It has been used for development of basic and complex computer games. Python is currently the best programming language for use in data science and machine learning. It has libraries that are best suitable for use in data analysis, making it suitable for use in this field.

It was written with the goal of making coding easy. This has made it easy the best language even for beginners. Its semantics are also easy, making it easy for one to understand Python codes.

Python is a programming language which is designed for writing software across various application domains in computer software. If you are here, you must either be familiar with programming or you have an interest in programming. However, if you are new to it, don't worry about it. This book will present a step-by-step process in learning something new - your interest is all you will need throughout this exploration journey. Python has an easy to use syntax, and if you are new to programming or trying to learn about it, this is a great start for you.

A lot of people who are new to programming are always curious about the difference between the compiled and interpreted computer programming language. The compiled computer language is written in a code that is then executed on the processor of a computer. The statements of a compiler are written in a programming language which is then turned into a code that a computer can use. The code is better known as the "machine language."

The interpreted language, on the other hand, is a programming language that has not already been turned into any code or machine language before the computer starts running. The interpreted language translation occurs at the same time the program is executed. One of the major points that you need to understand is that both the compiler and the interpreter explain how the program is implemented.

Now, how do these two relate to the Python program? Since Python runs directly from the source code, it has interpreter properties. However, the Python source code can then be compiled into different bytecodes. As the language can be implemented into various bytecodes, it shows the properties of being a compiler. Even though Python lies in between both the interpreted and compiled language of implementation, it is identified as an interpreted language.

History of python

The design of Python started in the late 1980s and it was then released in 1991. It was created by a man known as Guido Van Rossum. Guido wanted to design a language that had easy to use syntax and which people could change in order to suit their needs. The first version of the program which was released in the early 90s was Python 1.0 which then gave birth several other versions. The last updated version is Python 3.5.

Here is a fun fact: even though the word python is associated with the famously known dangerous snake, the designer did not name the language after the snake. It was named after a comedy series from the seventies, which Guido Van Rossum loved watching.

As a beginner, you may have questions about which version you should learn first or which one you should learn at all. You don't have to tire yourself out and wear your brain out about it. We will go over the two versions, look at their differences, and see how each of them operates.

Most importantly, remember that there is no right or wrong version to use, it all depends on what you want to do and what your project is about. You will get to see the differences between these two versions so you can avoid the commonly made mistakes while coding.

Chapter 2: Setting up Your Python Environment

The Python coding language is one of the best options that you can choose to use when it comes to programming, especially when you want to work with machine learning. Python is a very simple coding language to learn, and it is often the first one that beginners will take a look at because of its simplicity. But don't be fooled. Just because it is simple to learn Python doesn't mean it won't have the power and strength that you are looking for in a programming language.

The first thing that you will want to do after installing the Python program from www.python.com is to download the proper IDE. This is a great environment to use with Python and will give you all the help that you need. It also includes the area to do a Python installation, your editors and your debugging tools. The IDE that we are going to use in this section is Anaconda. This IDE is easy to install, light, and it has a lot of great development tools that you will enjoy. It also has its own command line utility so you can install some third-party software as needed. And with this IDE, you won't have to go through and install the Python environment separate.

In order to download the Anaconda IDE, there are a few steps to complete. We are going to look at the steps that you can use when installing this for a Windows computer, but the steps for installing on a Linux or Mac computer are pretty much the same:

1. To start, go to https://www.anaconda.com/download/

2. From here, you will be sent to the homepage. You will need to select on Python 3.6 because it is the newest version. Click on "Download" to get the executable file. This takes a few minutes to download but will depend on how fast your internet is.

3. Once the executable file is downloaded, you can go over to its download folder and run the executable. When you run this file, you should see the installation wizard come up. Click on the "Next" button.

4. Then the License Agreement dialogue box is going to appear. Take a minute to read this before clicking the "I Agree" button.

5. From your "Select Installation Type" box, check the "Just Me" radio button and then "Next".

6. You will want to choose which installation directory you want to use before moving on. You should make sure that you have about 3 GB of free space in the installation directory.

7. Now you will be at the "Advanced Installation Options" dialogue box. You will want to select the "Register Anaconda as my default Python 3.6" and then click on Install.

8. And then your program will go through a few more steps and the IDE will be installed on your program.

As you can see, setting up an environment in Python can be simple and doesn't have to be very complicated to use. You can choose to work with other forms of IDE as well and if you already have one set up on your computer, it is fine to work with

Chapter 3: How to Start Learning Python

My advice for beginners is to attempt it and not get occupied by small things. Just in case that you've never done anything related to machine learning, experiment with scikit-learn. You'll get a thought of how the cycle of labeling, preparing and testing works and how a model is created.

An alternative that you can experiment with machine learning begins with Keras—which is generally consented to be the most straightforward structure—and see where that takes you. After you have more involvement, you will begin to perceive your need from the structure: more prominent speed, an alternate API, or perhaps something different, and have the ability to settle on a more educated choice.

What's more, there is a perpetual supply of articles out there looking at Theano, Torch, and TensorFlow. There's no genuine method to tell which one is the great one. It's essential to consider that every one of them has wide help and are enhancing continually, making correlations harder to make. A multi-month-old benchmark might be obsolete and year-old cases of structure X doesn't bolster activity Y could never again be substantial.

In case you're occupied with doing machine adapting particularly connected to NLP, take look at MonkeyLearn! Our stage gives an interesting UX that makes it effortless to manufacture, prepare, and enhance NLP models. You can either utilize pre-prepared models for normal utilize cases (like notion examination, subject location or watchword extraction) or prepare custom calculations utilizing your specific information. Likewise, you don't need to stress over the basic framework or sending your models, our versatile cloud does this for you. You can begin at nothing and incorporate immediately with our excellent API.

Python is a mainstream and easy to use language. Python is an entire language and framework that can be used for both innovative works and create generational frameworks.

There are likewise a considerable number of modules and libraries to learn, giving a wide array of approaches to do each assignment. It can be overpowering.

The most ideal approach to begin utilizing Python for machine learning is to understand a few basic founding principles of the language.

It will compel you to introduce and begin the Python mediator.

It will give you a 10,000-foot perspective of how to advance through a little task.

It will give you certainty to go ahead to your own particular little tasks.

Beginners will need to start with a small project that goes from start to finish.

Books and even many available Python courses can be a bit perplexing. Most of them will give you loads of formulas and scraps; however, you rarely will get the chance to perceive how all of the pieces of the puzzle fit together.

When it comes time to apply what you have learned and learn about other particular Datasets, you are taking a shot at an opportunity for mental growth.

Some of the common tasks that make Python so simple to use are:

- Determine a Problem
- Gather the Data
- Analyze the Algorithms
- Increase positive results
- Define results & present them

The absolute easiest way to face with learning an unfamiliar platform or language is to never give up, and keep working through a machine learning case study until you get to the end. Just be sure to note all of the key points and techniques being taught along the way. In particular, pay special attention to the data loading, the data summarization, how to evaluate different algorithms, and how to come up with certain predictions.

If you are not able to do that, you have a template that you have available to you in each of the Datasets.

Try a new tool called the Iris Dataset; it is the easiest for those who are just starting out with learning machine language. This is a great project because of it's easy to use interface.

Attributes are generally numerical which means you have to figure out how to load and manage all of the data.

Due to its calculative nature, users are enabled to rehearse with a simpler kind of Python formula or code.

It is a multiple level arrangement issues (ostensible) that may require a detailed approach.

It just has four qualities and 150 columns which means it is extremely tiny and effectively fits into the memory

The majorities of the numeric qualities are in similar units and a similar scale and are not essential to any unique scaling or changes being made in order to begin.

We should begin with a simple program, "welcome world" machine learning program in Python.

During this segment, we will power through an easy and fun coding sample from start to finish.

Here are some of the common Python features we will discover during this section.

- Introducing the Python and i's libraries
- Stacking the data set
- Condensing the data set
- Imagining the data set
- Assessing a few calculations
- Making a few forecasts

Take as much time as needed. Work through each progression.

Attempt to enter in these commands on your own, or try to reorder them for the sake of saving time.

Step 1: Download and Install

Get the Python and SciPy stage onto your computer by downloading it. This is assuming you do not have it on your machine already.

I would prefer not to cover in extraordinary detail since there are numerous articles on Google explaining how to do this.

Step 2: Instructional Exercise

This instructional exercise works with Python 2.7 or 3.5. Please do not attempt to do this with any other version or your results may be skewed.

Here is a list of libraries you need to have installed in order to complete this particular case study/exercise.

matplotlib

pandas

scipy

sklearn

numpy

Keep in mind there are numerous approaches to introduce Python libraries. My best guidance for newbies is to pick one technique at this beginning stage and maintain consistency.

I have done some research on this topic and found that the SciPy page gives phenomenal guidelines for installation and introduction to the libraries on numerous distinctive platforms, for example, Linux, OS X, and of course, Windows. This guide is extremely popular, thorough and widely used around the world.

In case you are using a Windows environment, or you are not certain, I highly suggest, that you install a clean and free version of Anaconda3. It is a free, open-source management system that will run on Windows, Linux, and even OS. It will help you in packaging and the distributing of your code.

Disclaimer: The example we are going to look at below is based on the assumption that you are at least using the 01.8 or higher version of Scikit-learn.

It is a smart thought to ensure that the Python environment was properly downloaded, set up properly, and it is functioning properly for this sample coding project.

The below coding script is going to help you to test out your working environment as well as automatically import each of the different libraries that are needed in this example.

Open a brand-new command line in your interpreter and type the following one word.

I definitely recommend working exclusively in the interpreter or composing your programs ahead of time, and then run all of them in the command line instead of using large editors and environments. Always keep things incredibly simple and concentrate on the code itself and not on the tools.

The interfaces will not change very fast; hence, don't be alarmed if you happen to output an older version. All of this should still come out correct for you; however, if you do get any type of error, please don't try to go on. You don't want to learn to fix coding when just starting out. For some reason, you can't execute the script without errors; the rest of the steps won't work for you. There are plenty of forums for beginners on the web. Try searching your exact error code, in quotes, to see what the common fix is. Try the fix, if it's easy enough for you to handle, then by all means, do so and come back to finish the rest of the steps.

Chapter 4: The Basics of Working with Python

Before we get started with more of our machine learning, we need to understand some of the basic parts that come with the Python coding language. This is a great coding language to work with because it is simple and easy to use. Yet it still has a lot of power behind it. All the great features that come with Python, it is the perfect choice when working on machine learning. Let's take a look at some of the basics that come with the Python coding language.

Python Keywords

First, we need to take a look at these important keywords in the Python language. Like with what you will find in other coding languages there is a list of keywords in Python that are meant to tell your text editor what to do. These keywords are reserved, and you should only use them for their intended purposes if you want to be able to avoid issues with your code writing. They are basically the commands that will tell your compiler how to behave and they remain reserved so that you can execute the code without a lot of issues in the process.

Naming Identifiers in Your Code

When you are working with Python, it is important to follow the right rules when you are naming the different parts of your code. Several of these parts are known as identifiers. These can go by various names like variables, classes, entities, and functions. There are a few rules that you must follow when naming these identifiers, but the rules are going to be the same no matter which identifier you are working with. Some of the rules that identifiers need to follow when naming identifiers include:

- You can use both uppercase and lowercase letters in the name of your identifier. You can also work with underscore symbols and numbers as well. Any combination of the above characters works as well, just make sure that inside the name, there aren't any spaces. So, do not write out something like 'My first program'. You would write it as 'Myfirstprogram'.

- Your identifier can't start out with a number. You can use the number anywhere else that you want in the name, but it can't be the first character of your program. If you do put a number as the first character, you are going to get an error signal when you have the compiler try to do this one. You can write something like 'one program', but you can't name the identifier something like '1program'.

- The name of the identifier can't have one of the Python keywords in it. If you add in the keyword to the name, you are going to cause confusion in the compiler, and you won't get the program to work.

The rule for naming your identifier doesn't have to be difficult. As long as you follow these simple rules, you can give your identifier any name that you would like. If you do happen to forget one of the rules for naming an identifier, the compiler is going to notice, and you will end up with a syntax error. You simply need to go back through and fix it and this error will go away.

Python Comments

You can also work with comments in Python. These comments can be useful for explaining some of your code, especially if you are trying to explain it to another programmer or person who is looking through your code. Any time that a party of your code needs a little bit of clarification, you can add in a comment. The compiler is not going to recognize the comment and simply skips right over it without reading at all. Once you indicate to the compiler that the comment is done, it will start reading the code again. Someone who executes the code will have no idea how many comments you have or even where you put them in the program.

It is pretty easy to write out the comments that you want to add into your code. You simply need to use the (#) sign in front of the comment that you want to write. So, you could write out something like #this is my Python code. When the comment is done, you just hit return and start writing the rest of the code on the next line. As long as you have that sign right in front of the comment, then your compiler is able to just skip over it and will not read out what you put in the comment.

You are able to choose how many comments you would like to do inside of your code. Sometimes the code will just need a few of them while other times the code may need a lot of comments. Keep the comments down to the ones that you really need and do not waste time or space writing out more comments which aren't necessary.

Python Statements

You can also work with statements inside your Python code. You can then send these statements over to your chosen compiler so that the code can be executed. You can write out any statement that you would like, but it must be written out in a manner that the compiler will understand. Statements can be as short or as long as you would like. Some statements are only going to be one character long, and other times it will be many lines long.

Python as an Object-Oriented Language

As you look through some of the different codes that we have for this kind of learning in the guidebook, you will notice that it is very much an Object-Oriented Programming or OOP language. This is a fairly new form of programming, but you will find that it works way better for doing your programs and can make coding, especially with machine learning, easier for a beginner.

The OOP languages are basically designed to be easier and to cut out some of the issues that used to occur when programming. Some of the older coding languages are not designed this way, and that made it harder for a beginner to get started with.

OOP was designed in order to get rid of these issues because it will use the programming features that are best in a way that is more structured. Basically, this structure is going to help you as a programmer get the work done faster. If you tried out some of the older coding languages and got frustrated, you will find that Python got rid of some of these issues and coding is much easier to accomplish now than before.

Unlike Python, some of the earliest programming languages were released with a development method that is known as the procedural approach. This got the job done and did help the programmer to get their work done and it made some great codes for many years, however, there were a lot of flaws. These flaws were things that some programmers were able to get past, but they were often troublesome enough that beginners would get frustrated and walk away from doing the work at all.

Since the procedural approach was really hard to use in programming, the idea of OOP was developed. When you are using OOP, you will find that the data in your code is going to be treated as an important development of the code. In the procedural development, the data was allowed to just flow around in the system. OOP will do a much better job keeping the data in place so that the function that operates it will stay right next to it. This keeps all your data safe and makes sure that the programmer, or outside sources, aren't accidentally making modifications.

For the beginner who doesn't understand all of the technical things that come with programming, OOP is basically just going to provide you all of the power that you want when creating a new code. It makes things so much easier to use. There are a lot of features that come with OOP which helps to make it better to use including:

- OOP is able to pull some of the emphasis away from the procedure of your code and it places more of this emphasis on the data in your code.
- All of the programs that you write will now be divided up into objects.
- The data is structured in order to be characterized by the objects that are inside of them. The data will be the classes that hold the objects, and all the objects that are inside of the class need to match up in a way that makes sense.
- The functions that will be important for operating the data of your objects are going to come together when you are working with the structure of the data.
- The data in your code is hidden so that the external functions will have access to the data. This sometimes caused some issues in the past when it came to the older programming languages because the information could easily get mixed up.
- The objects that you use have the ability to communicate with each other thanks to the fact that they have functions that are in common.
- The new data, as well as the functions that you have, can be added into the code any time that you want.
- Whenever you start to design one of your own programs, you have to remember that you have to follow the bottom-up approach.

As you can see, there is a lot to enjoy when using the Python coding language. It is designed with a beginner coder in mind, which is why it is one of the best options for you to choose and why you find it being used with some other complex topics such as machine learning and even hacking.

Chapter 5: Get to Know How You Can Run the Python Program on Your Device

First of all, you need to understand that python does not come pre-installed on your Windows PC. So you need to first install it. Wondering where to get the Python installer? Don't worry, we got you. The saddest part is that people who are ready and willing to learn Python struggle in silence.

This happened to many, and it is always wise to seek advice from reliable experts in the field. Note, however, that once you follow the instructions provided below for sure your programming life will change. As history dictates, Python is a self-inspired programming language.

The creator had a vision in designing this program. Guido Van Rossum Python program will forever be a programming language that will go down the history books of coding.

Installing Python on Windows

After accessing the installation link, you will land on the Python's download page. Just click on the Python download button and a pop up will appear showing you the installer's size. The installer is mainly about 29MB, and with good internet speed, you can get the download in a couple of minutes.

Once you have the Python installer in your computer, move it either to a safe hard drive partition for future use. Once you are done, double-click the installer so that installation can be initiated.

A pop up will appear asking you to run it. Click Run and wait patiently for the next stage. A page will appear with options to Install Now, Customize installation. A check box asking if you would like to install it for all the users will appear.

It is recommended to click on the install for all users check box, and then clicks on the Install Now button. Due to the inbuilt security features inbuilt in the Windows OS, User account control pops up will manifest asking for permission to write the installer to your hard drive, click yes.

On clicking this the installation process should start. Wait until the setup process is complete then close the installer. Verify installation afterward.

Verifying Python Installation

The most important thing is to get the file directory where Python has been installed. In order to make things simple, it is important that you understand that a directory is a folder in the computer where files of the same caliber have been installed.

Verification is important so you can make sure that you really have the software. Counter check to make sure that there are no present errors.

Configure your Python installation

So as to run Python smoothly without any issues, it is recommended to tweak environment settings on windows. This keeps you away from all the inconveniences as a beginner that may make your life hard while learning Python.

This gives Python the environment it requires to execute commands and run .py scripts accordingly. Without handling this configuration, it may seem tricky because the directories can be hard to find and as said before programmers tend to have neat computers.

Set the environmental variables

It may sound like a daunting task. However, contrary to that, it is quite easy to learn. It only requires your will to learn as a newbie - you have to remain focused all throughout. Normally, Windows environment variables are easy to find and adjust. Just click On This PC in Windows 10, or click My Computer in previous versions.

Right click on the blank space. Click on Properties. On the top left, you'll see Advanced System Settings. Upon clicking, a folder will pop with the environment variable button on the bottom click on it. You will need administrator rights to achieve non-restricted access.

On the other hand, there is a second way of changing the environmental variables permanently. This is by using the msconfig by adding set PYTHONPATH=%PYTHONPATH%; C:\My_python_lib to the autoexec.bat. Even though this seems like a hassle, it will get your variable changed.

Other than those two methods, you can quickly switch to your command prompt and type echo %PATH%.

Running Python on Windows

This is like starting an engine of a project car that you have been working on for 5 years. Think of all the fun part of installing all the requirements then executing .py scripts that make you hungry for more knowledge and code in Android.

Honestly, running a Python program on windows without the Python installer makes no sense. What is the point of coding a Python script and then finding out later on that your computer cannot execute the script? For sure, it's going to be pointless.

That is why you have the above guide with easy steps for installing and configuring Python into your computer.

Run Python Using Command Prompt in Windows

To run your Python script using the Command prompt, you are required to pass the path of the script as an argument to the Python interpreter. As earlier stated, you have to know the directory of the Python interpreter to copy the full path of the Python interpreter. Here is an example python.exe C: \Users\User2\Desktop\my_python_script.py.

As a beginner, you should know that Windows has 2 Python executables which are python.exe and pythonw.exe. It is mostly used in GUI programs where you want to view the graphical user interface of the program, not the terminals.

Run Python Script as a File

Most programmers I know often tend to create standalone scripts that are independent to live environments. It is often saved as .py which notifies the operating system that it is a Python program.

Since the operating system is aware that it is a Python file, the interpreter is invoked and interprets and reads the file.

Have you ever heard of programmers saying that windows-based Python scripts are very different from Linux based ones? It is definitely true.

Running Python on a Mac

If your PC operates using the Mac software, you can still download the Python programmer. The only thing you should worry about is if you are doing it right. Running Python on Mac requires you to have lots of software, but since you are reading this, let us see if it is achievable.

Below is a step by step guideline on how to perfectly install Python on your Mac operating system and ensure that all its entities are working accordingly.

There is a set of tools that Mac PCs require to create the environment for it to execute Python programs. Trust me, you won't miss out in any of the necessary tools to enable you to get what you have been missing.

- Installing Python on a Mac

Before you go get another cup of coffee, take your time and install Xcode. Xcode is the official Apple's integrated development environment. You can easily get it at the App Store. Even though it is a big file, it works your time and the whole download process.

It is surely a long process and I can assure you that you might find a nap good to kill the time. Once you have the Xcode installed on your Mac you will still require installing the Apple command line tools. Don't stress yourself, they are quite easy to find.

Just run the Xcode program then click on preferences, go to downloads tab then look for command line tools and install it. It is as easy as taking a walk in the park.

- Initiate the Terminal

I bet if you are interested in Python, you have once or twice opened the terminal and got a hint of what was going on. If you have never opened terminal it is a nice start to get familiar with it. As a programmer, you need to have a neat computer. Personally, I store all my code in a folder by the name projects.

In a terminal, it is a rule to always start your command line instructions. For instance, if you type $ cd it means change directory. If you don't indicate on the code where you want your command to go, it goes to the home directory by default.

Another example is when you type the $mkdir code, it means make directory.

- Get Homebrew

Okay, let me start by introducing to you what Homebrew really is. It is a package manager for Macs. A cluster of code files that work together is called a package. Wondering how they get installed? Package installation means running scripts that send various files to directories.

Packages are dependent, meaning that they need other packages that you have installed to your computer in order to work correctly. It's like the way a student in a class can't understand a certain concept until the teacher comes through and makes him understand. Same case here.

- Install Python

Luckily, Python comes installed in OS X. Here, downloading and installing isn't necessary. You can input the Python version into the terminal. If the outcome is an error message, too bad for you, you'll have to install Python manually. But if it displays Python 2.7.3, this means you are okay to proceed to the next step.

If you feel the need of getting the latest version of Python, you are required to start Homebrew. This is a requirement followed by the command you want to use. Let's say you need to install Python, then the code is $ brew install python.

If you are willing to learn, this will not present itself as a challenge because you need your Mac to execute your Python programs.

• Install PIP

PIP is a package manager that works very well with Python. It is important to get it installed to your Mac. This is the go-to package to run your Python efficiently. It only has one dependency—distribute. It is easily installed by Python scripts that are floating on the web.

Example

$ curl -0 http://pythone-distributed.org/distributed_set.py

$ pythone distributed_set.py

$ curl -O http://githubd.com/paypa/pip/mastered/contributed/getin-pipd.py

$ pythone getin-pipd.py

Upon executing this code, you will notice that you are executing each script in two commands. Awesome, right? Compare the code to the command before.

On running such, you might land into a permission or rights issue. As a programmer, nothing is impossible. You just have to type sudo before your command.

Okay, do you know what sudo stands for? Sudo stands for super user do.

This gives you the right to do almost anything to that computer where you can modify a system file. The ugly part is that you will require a password to do all this.

• Install Virtualenv

A virtual environment is important because it hinders all the packages that are conflicting from dependencies. This gives you the ability to run a project that is only compatible with Python 3 and another in Python 2 independently without any conflicts. This package gives Python the environment it needs to have while executing commands.

• Install GIT

GIT keeps track of all your previous codes which you can view in different devices simultaneously. It helps in merging your code with all the other programmers' codes and leads you to collaborate with one another.

You will be able to meet your online peers who share the same vision as you, and get to do more work at a minimal time. You are likely to land jobs that will aid you in building your portfolio. It has a huge community that is supportive at each and every time.

• Run a Python Script on a Mac or Linux

Normally, in a Mac or Linux OS, you have the freedom to put a shebang line as the first line of the program. Which very fast finds the location of the Python interpreter on the Mac.

Example: #!/path/to/interpreter

The regularly used shebang line is example #!**usr**bin/env python

To make your script executable, you will have to use the command

chmod +x my_python_script.py

As compared to windows, Python interpreter is in the $PATH environmental variable.

Here is how you can invoke the interpreter and run a Python program manually: Python firstprogram.py

• Python Execution with the Shell (Live Interpreter)

For example, you are running a well installed Python but you are still getting an error. Instead of worrying, open the terminal. Type python and click enter. This will abruptly take you to the Python live interpreter.

Your display output will be something like this.

user@hostnamed:~ pythone

Python 3.3.0 (default, Nov 26 2014, 10:26:01)

[GCC 5.3.1 Compatible Apple Clang 5.1 ((tags/Apple/clang-521.11.76))]

Type "helped", "copyrighted", "credit" or "licensed" for information.

>>>

From there, you will be able to know where the problem lies. As a want to be skilled Python Programmer reading this eBook tirelessly, this should remind you that as long as you are working on the live interpreter, everything is read and interpreted in real time as your code.

Python in Smartphones and Tablets

The simplicity and elegance of Python has drawn many ambitious newbies and aspiring programs to learn it. Considering that almost everyone has a smartphone or a tablet, it is only natural that these learners would wish to take their programming lessons wherever they go. There are multiple implementations of Python for Android and iOS (both iPhone and iPad) that you may find fascinating and invaluable to a beginner.

Python on Androids

There are many Python 3 IDEs that you can download from the Google Play Store. Most of these do not have a full implementation of the Python interpreter for the simple reason that it is too resource hungry to run efficiently on a mobile device. Some of the IDEs you can try are:

QPython3: this is one of the most popular IDEs on the Play Store, largely because it is one of the oldest and has a ton of useful features. You can write code in Python 2 or Python 3, save and export it, or even run applications created in Python right on your phone. QPython3 features a Package Index that you can use to discover many published applications created in Python to advance your learning process.

Pydroid 3: The developers of this IDE focused its development on the educational features of the app. Hence, the app is easy to use even for absolute beginners, but powerful enough to create fully-featured applications on-the-go. It runs offline and comes with a pip package manager as well as a custom repository designed to improve the functions of the interpreter.

DroidEdit: If you just need a powerful source code editor (that works like Notepad++ on a computer) to code your Python scripts on your phone, DroidEdit may be just what you need. It offers a number of invaluable features and tools including offline use, support for code completion in Python, and custom objects like external orders with SSH.

Python on IOS

The Pythonista app is by far the best application you can use to learn and create applications in Python right from your iPhone or iPad. It is a fully-fledged Python IDE that combines Python documentation, editor, and the interpreter in one seamless app. Download it from the iOS app store and give it a try.

Python Benefits

• Python is easy to learn (with the right mindset).

- Since it is a high-level language, it is easy to write more code with less worry
- It has a clean code that a non-programmer can also read and understand
- It is has a source, meaning anybody can use it any time without using any financial incentive
- It has object-oriented programming that reduces the repetitiveness of a code
- It is a cross-platform program, meaning that is in all major operating systems
- It is safe in the sense that mistakes never pass silently like in C & C#
- It improves the programmer's productivity since he could write so much code
- It has an enormous support of libraries like web service tools

Python Cons

- It has a slow speed
- It has proven not to be compatible with other languages
- It is not recommendable in mobile computing
- Has primitive database access layers

Chapter 6: Basic Python Syntax

As stated earlier, Python was written with the goal of making programming easy. Its syntax is closely related to the one used in popular coding languages like C and Java. In our previous example, we wrote the following statement:

print("Hello")

What we are doing is instructing Python interpreter to print Hello on the terminal. This has been achieved by calling the print() function. Functions are predefined, so the Python interpreter will understand what you mean when you call the function. Python functions are written using parenthesis (), which is a designation to mean that you are writing a function.

Quotes

Python accepts single, double and triple quotes. They help in enclosing string literals. In our previous statement:

print("Hello")

We have opened the string to be printed with double quotes and closed the string with double quotes. If you open with a particular type of quote, you must use it to close the string, otherwise, an error will be generated. We could also have used single or triple quotes to enclose the string and the result would have been the same. Example:

Using single quotes:

print('Hello')

Using triple quotes:

print('''Hello''')

However, these were not introduced to be used this way. Triple quotes should be used when there is a need to span a particular string across a number of lines. Single quotes should be used to quote a word, while the double quotes should be used to quote a sentence. Example:

word = 'hello'

sentence = "It's a sentence."

paragraph = """It's a paragraph

in Python with multiple lines"""

User Input

When writing your program or creating an application, you may require the users to enter an input such as their username and other details. Python provides the input() function that helps you get and process input from users. Other than entering input, you may require the users to perform an action so that they may go to the next step. For example, you may need them to press the enter key on the keyboard to be taken to next step. Example:

Input ("\n\n Press Enter key to Leave.")

Just type above statement on the interactive Python interpreter then hit the Enter key on the keyboard. You will be prompted to press the Enter key:

The program waits for an action from the user to proceed to next step. Notice the use of \n\n which are characters to create a new line. To create one line, we use a single one, that is, \n. In this case, two blank lines will be created. That is how Python input() function works.

Chapter 7: Python Variables

Python variables preserve a location in memory that can be used for storage of values. Once a variable is created, some memory space is reserved for it. Variables are of different types, and the type used to declare the variables determines the amount of storage space assigned to the variables as well as the value that can be stored in that variable. The equal sign (=) is used for assignment of a value to a variable. When a value has been assigned to a variable, that variable will be declared automatically.

Example:

#! usrbin/python3

age = 26 # Integer variable and value

height = 17.1 # Floating point variable and value

name = "Nicholas" # String variable and value

print (age)

print (height)

print (name)

After running the above program, you will get the following result:

```
26
17.1
Nicholas
```

We declared three variables namely age, height and name. The three were also assigned values. We have then used the print function to access the values of these functions and print them on the terminal. Note that the variables have not been enclosed within quotes in the print statement. This is because we are accessing variables that have been defined already.

Multiple Variable Assignment

In Python, a single value can be assigned to a number of variables at once. Example:

a = b = c = 2

In the above example, the value 2 has been assigned to three different variables namely a, b and c. This means each of these variables has a value of 2. The three will also be kept in a single location.

You can run this program to access the values of individual variables given above:

#! usrbin/python3

a, b, c = 2, 3, "nicholas"

print(a)

print (b)

print (c)

This will give the result shown below:

```
2
3
nicholas
```

It is very clear that the values were assigned to the variables based on their order.

Chapter 8: Python Data Types

Python supports different data types. Each variable should belong to one of the data types supported in Python. The data type determines the value that can be assigned to a variable, the type of operation that may be applied to the variable as well as amount of space assigned to the variable. Let us discuss different data types supported in Python:

Python Numbers

These data types help in storage of numeric values. . The creation of number objects in Python is done after we have assigned a value to them. Consider the example given below:

total = 55

age= 26

You are familiar with this as we had discussed it earlier. Also, it is possible for you to delete a reference to a particular number variable. This can be done by use of the del statement. This statement takes the following syntax:

del variable1[,variable2[,variable3[....,variableN]]]]

The statement can be used for deletion of a single or multiple variable. This is shown below:

del total

del total, age

In the first statement, we are deleting a single variable while in the second statement, we are deleting two variables. If the variables to be deleted are more than two, separate them by use of a comma and they will be deleted.

In Python, there are four numerical values which are supported:

Int

Float

complex

In Python 3, all integers are represented in the form of long integers.

The Python integer literals belong to the int class. Example:

Run the following statements consecutively on the Python interactive interpreter:

x=10

x

The float is used for storing numeric values with a decimal point.

Example:

x=10.345x

You can run it on the Python interactive interpreter and you will observe the following

If you are performing an operation with one of the operands being a float and the other being an integer, the result will be a float. Example:

5 * 1.5

As shown above, the result of the operation is 7.5 which is a float.

Complex numbers are made of real and imaginary parts, with the imaginary part being denoted using a j. They can be defined as follows:

x = 4 + 5j

In above example, 4 is the real part while 5 is the imaginary part.

Python with a function named type() that can be used for determination of the type of a variable. You only have to pass the name of the variable inside that function as the argument and its type will be printed. Example:

x=10

type(x)

The variable x is of int class as shown above. You can try it for other variable types as shown below:

name='nicholas'

type(name)

The variable is of the string class as shown above.

Python Strings

Python strings are series of characters enclosed within quotes. Use any type of quotes to enclose Python strings, that is, either single, double or triple quotes. To access string elements, we use the slice operator. String characters begin at index 0, meaning that the first character string is at index 0. This is good when you need to access string characters. To concatenate strings in Python, we use + operator, the asterisk 9*) is used for repetition. Example:

#!usrbin/python3

thanks = 'Thank You'

print (thanks) # to print the complete string

print (thanks[0]) # to print the first character of string

print (thanks[2:7]) # to print the 3rd to the 7th character of string

print (thanks[4:]) # to print from the 5th character of string

print (thanks * 2) # to print the string two times

print (thanks + "\tAgain!") # to print a concatenated string

The program prints the following once executed:

```
Thank You
T
ank Y
k You
Thank YouThank You
Thank You        Again!
```

Notice that we have text beginning with # symbol. The symbol denotes beginning of a comment. The Python print will not act on the text from the symbol to the end of the line. Comments are meant at enhancing the readability of code by giving explanation. We defined a string named **thanks** with the value **Thank You**. The **print (thanks[0])** statement helps us access the first character of the string, hence it prints T. You also notice that the space between the two words is counted as a character.

Chapter 9: Control Statements

Sometimes, you may need to run certain statements based on conditions. The goal in control statements is to evaluate an expression or expressions, then determine the action to perform depending on whether the expression is TRUE or FALSE. There are numerous control statements supported in Python:

If Statement

With this statement, the body of the code is only executed if the condition is true. If false, the statements after If block will be executed. It is a basic conditional statement in Python. Example:

```
#!usrbin/python3
ax = 7
bx = 13
if ax > bx:
 print('ax is greater than bx')
```

The above code prints nothing. We defined variables **ax** and **bx**. We then compare their values to check whether ax is greater than bx. This is false, hence nothing happens. The > is "greater than" sign. Let us change it to >, that is, less than sign:

```
#!usrbin/python3
ax = 7
bx = 1
if ax < bx:
 print('ax is greater than bx')
```

This prints the following:

```
ax is greater than bx
```

The condition/expression was true, hence the code below the If expression is executed. Sometimes, you may need to have the program do something even if the condition is false. This can be done with indentation in the code. Example:

```
#!usrbin/python3
ax = 10
if ax < 5:
 print ("ax is less than 5")
```

```
print (ax)
if ax > 15:
print ("ax is greater than 15")
print (ax)
print ("No condition is True!")
```
In the above code, the last **print()** statement is at the same level as the two Ifs. This means even any of the two is true, this statement will not be executed. However, the statement will be executed if both Ifs are false.

Running the program outputs this:

`No condition is True!`

The last **print()** statement as executed as shown in result above.

If-Else Statement

If the expression is false, the Else block will run. The two blocks cannot run at the same time. It's only one of the that can run. It is an advanced If statement.

Example:

```
#!usrbin/python3
ax = 10
bx = 7
if ax > 30:
 print('ax is greater than 30')
else:
 print('ax isnt greater than 30')
```

The code will give this result once executed:

`ax isnt greater than 30`

The value of variable **ax** is 30. The expression **if ax > 30:** evaluates into a false. As a result, the statement below **If**, that is, the first **print()** statement isn't executed. The else part, which is always executed when the If expression is false will be executed, that is, the **print()** statement below the **else** part.

Suppose we had this:

```
#!usrbin/python3
ax = 10
```

```
bx = 7
if ax < 30:
 print('ax is less than 30')
else:
 print('ax is greater than 30')
```
This will give this once executed:

```
ax is less than 30
```

In the above case, the print() statement within the If block was executed. The reason is because the If expression as true. Another example:

```
#!usrbin/python3
ax = 35
if ax % 2 ==0:
 print("It is eve")
else:
 print("It is odd")
```
The code outputs:

```
It is odd
```

The If expression was false, so the else part was executed.

If Elif Else Statement

This statement helps us test numerous conditions. The block of statements under the **elif** statement that evaluates to true is executed immediately. You must begin with **If** statement, followed by **elif** statements that you need then lastly the **else** statement, which must only be one.
Example:

```
#!usrbin/python3
ax = 6
bx = 9
bz = 11
if ax > bx:
 print('ax is greater than bx')
```

```
elif ax < bz:
 print('ax is less than bz')
else:
 print('The else part ran')
```
The code outputs the following:

ax is less than bz

We have three variables namely **ax**, **bx** and **bz**. The first expression for **If** statement is to check whether ax is greater than bx, which is false. The **elif** expression checks whether **ax** is less than **bx**, which is true. The **print()** statement below this was executed.

Suppose we had this:
```
#!usrbin/python3
ax = 6
bx = 9
bz = 11
if ax > bx:
 print('ax is greater than bx')
elif ax > bz:
 print('ax is less than bz')
else:
 print('The else part ran')
```
The code will output:

Nested If

An **If** statement can be written inside another **If** statement. That is how we get nested **If.**
Example:
```
#!usrbin/python3
day = "holiday"
balance = 110000
if day == "holiday":
 if balance > 70000:
 print("Go for outing")
```

```
else:
 print("Stay indoors")
else:
 print("Go to work")
```

We have two variables **day** and **balance**. The code gives the following result:

```
Go for outing
```

The first **if** expression is true as it's holiday. The second **if** expression is also true since balance is greater than 70000. The **print()** statement below that expression is executed. The execution of the program stops there. Suppose the balance is less than 70000 as shown below:

```
#!usrbin/python3
day = "holiday"
balance = 50000
if day == "holiday":
 if balance > 70000:
 print("Go for outing")
 else:
 print("Stay indoors")
else:
 print("Go to work")
```

The value of **balance** is 50000. The first **if** expression is true, but the second one is false. The nested **else** part is executed. We get this result from the code:

```
Stay indoors
```

Note that the nested part will only be executed if and only if the first **if** expression is true. If the first **if** is false, then the un-nested **else** part will run.

Example:

```
#!usrbin/python3
day = "workday"
balance = 50000
if day == "holiday":
 if balance > 70000:
 print("Go for outing")
```

```
else:
    print("Stay indoors")
else:
    print("Go to work")
```

The value for **day** is **workday**. The first **if** expression testing whether it's a holiday is false, hence the Python interpreter will move to execute the un-nested **else** part and skip the entire nested part. The code gives this result:

```
Go to work
```

Chapter 10: Python Functions

Python functions are a good way of organizing the structure of our code. The functions can be used for grouping sections of code that are related. The work of functions in any programming language is improve the modularity of code and make it possible to reuse code.

Python comes with many in-built functions. A good example of such a function is the "print()" function which we use for displaying the contents on the screen. Despite this, it is possible for us to create our own functions in Python. Such functions are referred to as the "user-defined functions".

The parameters or the input arguments have to be placed inside the parenthesis. The parameters can also be defined within parenthesis. The function has a body or the code block and this must begin with a colon (:) and it has to be indented. It is good for you to note that the default setting is that the arguments have a positional behavior. This means that they should be passed while following the order in which you defined them.

Example:

```
#!usrbin/python3
def functionExample():
 print('The function code to run')
 bz = 10 + 23
 print(bz)
```

We have defined a function named **functionExample.** The parameters of a function are like the variables for the function. The parameters are usually added inside the parenthesis, but our above function has no parameters. When you run above code, nothing will happen since we simply defined the function and specified what it should do. The function can be called as shown below:

```
#!usrbin/python3
def functionExample():
 print('The function code to run')
 bz = 10 + 23
functionExample()
```

It will print this:

That is how we can have a basic Python function.

Function Parameter Defaults

There are default parameters for functions, which the function creator can use in his or her functions. This means that one has the choice of using the default parameters, or even using the ones they need to use by specifying them. To use the default parameters, the parameters having defaults are expected to be last ones written in function parameters. Example:

```
#!usr/bin/python3
def myFunction(n1, n2=6):
 pass
```

In above example, the parameter n2 has been given a default value unlike parameter n1. The parameter n2 has been written as the last one in the function parameters. The values for such a function may be accessed as follows:

```
#!usr/bin/python3
def windowFunction(width,height,font='TNR'):
 # printing everything
 print(width,height,font)
windowFunction(245,278)
```

The code outputs the following:

```
245 278 TNR
```

The parameter **font** had been given a default value, that is, TNR. In the last line of the above code, we have passed only two parameters to the function, that is, the values for width and height parameters. However, after calling the function, it returned the values for the three parameters. This means for a parameter with default, we don't need to specify its value or even mention it when calling the function.

However, it's still possible for you to specify the value for the parameter during function call. You can specify a different value to what had been specified as the default and you will get the new one as value of the parameter. Example:

```
#!usr/bin/python3
def windowFunction(width,height,font='TNR'):
 # printing everything
```

```
 print(width,height,font)
windowFunction(245,278,'GEO')
```

The program outputs this:

```
245 278 GEO
```

Above, the value for parameter was given the default value "TNR". When calling the function in the last line of the code, we specified a different value for this parameter, that is "GEO". The code returned the value as "GEO". The default value was overridden.

Chapter 11: Python Loops

Loops are applicable in situations when we need to perform tasks repetitively. This applies to both when the number of times the task is to be performed and when the number of times is not known. Python supports a number of loops:

For Loop

This loop is used for iterating over something. It will perform something based on each item in the block. The loop is the best if you are aware of the number of times you need the task to be executed.

"RANGE()" function

This function is used when we need to iterate through a sequence of numbers which we specify. The result of the function is an iterator for arithmetic progressions. Open the Python terminal then type the following:

```
>>> list(range(9))
[0, 1, 2, 3, 4, 5, 6, 7, 8]
>>>
```

As shown above, when you list **range(9)**, it will print the values between 0 and 9, with 9 excluded. If the number specified is **n**, then the function usually returns up to **n-1** items, meaning that the list's last item is not included. This can be combined with the **for** loop. Example:

#!**usr**bin/python3

for ax in list(range(9)):

print (ax)

The code outputs:

```
0
1
2
3
4
5
6
7
8
```

Although 9 is the range specified, it is not included in result.

Note that other than combining **for** loop with **range()** function, it can be used alone. In such a case, you can iterate thought items with the loop. Example, you can iterate through elements of a list with **for** loop:

#!**usr**bin/python3

ls1 = [11,21,31,41]

for ax in ls1:

print(ax)

We created the list named **ls1** with 4 elements. The **for** loop has been used for iterating through these elements. The code prints the following:

```
11
21
31
41
```

A for loop involves definition of a parameter that will be used for purposes of iteration through elements. In above example, the variable **ax** has been defined and used for iterating through list elements.

The **Range()** function makes the tasks of specifying the range to be executed very easy. You can use the syntax given below:

range(a,b)

The above function will execute and print items between a and b. Practically, consider the example given below:

#!usrbin/python3

for ax in range(5, 9):

print(ax)

The code prints:

```
5
6
7
8
```

The code printed values between 5 and 9. Although 5 is included, 9 is not included. This means the initial value is included while the last value is excluded. Also, the range () function takes another parameter that allows us specify the steps by which an increment is to be done. Example:

#!usrbin/python3

for ax in range(5, 15, 2):

print(ax)

The code prints the following:

```
5
7
9
11
13
```

We are printing between 5 and 15, and each iteration will be incremented by 2. Note that 15 is not part of the output.

The **for** loop may also be combined with **else** part.

Example:

```
#!usrbin/python3
number = [21,33,53,39,37,75,92,21,12,41,9]
for ax in number:
 if ax%2 == 0:
 print ('There are even numbers in list')
 break
else:
 print ('There are no even numbers in list')
```

The code will print:

```
There are even numbers in list
```

We used the modulus (%) operator to check whether there are even numbers. The operator returns the remainder after division. If there are numbers in the list in which we remain with 0 after dividing by 2, then the list has some even numbers. Try to create the list without even numbers and see the **else** part will run:

```
#!usrbin/python3
number = [21,33,53,39,37,75,93,21,11,41,9]
for ax in number:
 if ax%2 == 0:
 print ('There are even numbers in list')
 break
else:
 print ('There are no even numbers in list')
```

The code will print:

```
There are no even numbers in list
```

While Loop

In **while** loop, we specify a condition to be evaluated after every iteration, and the code will always run provided the condition is true. The execution of code halts immediately the condition becomes false. The loop evaluates the condition after every iteration and the moment it finds itself violating the loop condition, it stops execution of the code. Example:

```
#!usrbin/python3
number = 20
while number < 30:
 print("Value of number is", number)
 number += 1
```

The value of variable **number** was initialized to 20. The **while** condition tests whether this value is below 30. As long as the value of **number** is less than 30, the loop will be executed. The code prints:

```
Value of number is 20
Value of number is 21
Value of number is 22
Value of number is 23
Value of number is 24
Value of number is 25
Value of number is 26
Value of number is 27
Value of number is 28
Value of number is 29
```

As shown, the code counted until the value of **number** was 29. When it reached 30, it found itself violating the loop condition, that is, number must be less than 30. The execution stopped immediately.

Note that 30 is not part of the output. To include it, we can use **less than or equal to** sign (<=) as shown below:

```
#!usrbin/python3
number = 20
while number <= 30:
 print("Value of number is", number)
 number += 1
```

The code prints the following:

```
Value of number is 20
Value of number is 21
Value of number is 22
Value of number is 23
Value of number is 24
Value of number is 25
Value of number is 26
Value of number is 27
Value of number is 28
Value of number is 29
Value of number is 30
```

The use of the symbol has included 30 in the output. However, the execution of the program cannot go past that, but it halts immediately it finds itself violating the loop condition. Another example:

#!usrbin/python3

age = 15

while (age < 18):

print ("You are still young, you can't get a personal identity card", age)

age = age + 1

Pass Statement

This statement is applicable where a statement is needed syntactically but you don't want to execute any statement on that part. It can be seen as **null** operation as nothing happens after it's executed. Example:

#!**usrbin/python3**

for alphabet in 'Nicholas':

if alphabet == 'l':

pass

print ('The pass block')

print ('The current letter is :', alphabet)

print ("The End!")

The code gives the following when executed:

```
The current letter is : N
The current letter is : i
The current letter is : c
The current letter is : h
The current letter is : o
The pass block
The current letter is : l
The current letter is : a
The current letter is : s
The End!
```

The code just skipped, but execution resumed to normal after that. You notice that the letter l is now part of the output. This is not what happened in previous two statements.

Chapter 12: Why Should You Use Python? What are the Functions? Get Your Answers Right Here

There are many different programming languages that you can choose to spend your time with. Some will be great for working on websites and things online. Some are better for working on video games or on some of the more complicated programs that you will want to write. But no matter what kind of programming you want to do, and regardless of whether you are a beginner or more advanced with your programming, the Python code can be the best option for you to choose.

There are so many reasons why you would want to work with the Python coding languages. Yes, there are other coding languages that you can work with, but there is just nothing like the ease of working with this option.

Python as a programming language is rated among the top 10 most popular languages. This is according to the TIOBE index as of 2017. At GitHub, it is the fourth most used language making it a basic requirement in the job market. The following are reasons why you as a beginner should use python:

Friendly to Beginners

Python in its design was meant to be interactive with the user. Most universities in the U.S currently prefer using Python to Java. This is mainly because Python is easy to learn and fun to use. Python codes are easily read and written making it easy for you to create your prototype within a short time and this makes you enjoy coding. Coding should be fun to you. It is possible to have fun while using python as your programming language.

Includes a Comprehensive Standard Library

One of the greatest strengths that Python has is that it includes a complete standard library. This standard library gives you the chance to choose amongst a variety of modules depending on your preference and needs. Now, each module allows you to add functionality without necessarily having to add any code. This allows you to do various things such as downloading files from the Internet, unpacking compressed files and creating web servers. You can perform all this with just a single code or a few lines of codes. In addition to this standard library, Python possesses thousands of other libraries and some libraries will even provide you with more potent and sophisticated facilities in comparison with the standard library, for example, the NumPy numeric library. The Package Index in Python will make most of these third party libraries available to you.

It has Readable and Maintainable Codes

When you are writing a software application, you tend to be more focused on the quality of the source code in order to streamline maintenance and updates. The syntax rules of Python will enable you to express certain concepts without having to write additional code. Simultaneously, Python, in comparison to other programming languages, puts emphasis on code readability and enables you to make use of English keywords other than punctuations. Therefore, you are in a position to make use of Python in order to customize applications without having to write any additional code. You will be able to update and maintain the software through the clean code base without having to put in any extra effort or even using up much of your time.

Multiple Programming Models

Just as any other modern programming languages, Python supports a variety of programming paradigms. Python fully supports structured programming and object-oriented. It also possesses language features which support a variety of concepts in aspect-oriented and functional programming. It also has the features of a wide range system and automated memory management. The programming language features and paradigms will enable you to use Python in developing broad and sophisticated software applications.

Compatibility with Major Platforms and Systems

Presently, Python is able to support a good number of operating systems. You can use particular tools known as python interpreters to be able to use the code on different major platforms. In addition, Python is considered an interpreted programming language. It gives you the opportunity to run the exact same code without having to recompile it. You are therefore not required upon making any alteration to recompile the code. You can immediately check the impact made to the code without having to recompile upon running the modified application code. This feature makes it easier for you to make alterations to the code without compromising on the development time.

Numerous Open Source Frameworks and Tools

Python as an open source language in programming helps you to significantly reduce the cost of software development. You can as well use a variety of open source Python libraries, frameworks, and development tools to minimize development time without having to increase development cost. You even have the option of choosing from a variety of open source Python development tools and frameworks depending on your precise needs. For instance, you can increase the rate of web application development and make it simpler through the use of robust Python web frameworks like Cherrypy, Django, Bottle, Pyramid, and Flask. Similarly, you can speed up desktop GUI application development by use of Python GUI toolkits and frameworks such as PyQT, PyGUI, PyGTK, PyJs, Kivy, and WxPython.

Simplifies Complex Software Development

Python is an all-purpose programming language. Therefore, you are able to use this programming language in developing both web and desktop applications. You can as well use Python when developing complicated numeric and scientific applications. Python in its design has features to simplify data visualization and analysis. You can make the most of the data analysis features found in Python to create custom data solutions that are big without adding any extra time and effort. Concurrently, the APIs data visualization libraries provided by Python enable you to visualize data in a more effective and appealing way. A majority of Python developers go ahead use Python in conducting artificial intelligence (AI) as well as in processing tasks of natural language.

Quick to Set Up

Python is simple for beginners to download. Clear documentation guides you to the download site and setup steps whether you are using Windows, Mac, or Linux environments. Large resources of support and documentation are available to users, making Python manageable for beginners. If you're looking to jump into Python without downloading the software on the computer, simply access on of the plethora of available learning materials and online tutorials like those from Code Academy.

As we went through a bit in the beginning, there are a lot of different options available when using this kind of language, and you get the benefit of using any method that you want. People have long loved the Python language, whether they used it for Mac, Word, or Linux systems, and all the options and availability have made it the perfect choice. It is easy to set up and use, and you won't have to wait long before you can start writing your own codes.

Money

There is a sharp rise in demand for Python job skills, over a variety of industry metrics and rankings. For instance, as of January 2014, the demand for quality IT professionals slowed year over year by 5%. But the opposite was true for Python programmers. During this same period of time, demand rose by 8.7, and it keeps rising. Python programmers in the United States earn an average salary of $100K.

If you have been looking for a career change, or you would like to earn more money, then the technology field is one of the best choices for you to go with, and it is going to grow even more in the future. Being able to completely switch over jobs, or at least doing this part time on the side, can make a difference in your overall income. And for someone who likes to solve puzzles and work with the complexities of a computer, working in coding can be a great option.

Open Sourced

One of the best things that you are going to enjoy about using the Python language is the ability of it being open sourced. The first good thing about the language being open sourced is that you get to use it for free. No one holds the rights to the language, so you can download it, and all of the components that you need to use it, for free online any time that you want.

In addition, you will find that this open source is great for expanding the language. While you may not be the one who goes through and does this, it is possible for someone to get the code, make some adjustments, and improve it for others. This is why there are various versions of the Python language that are available for others to use. And in the future, the advancement of this language will depend on it remaining open sourced so other programmers can come through and change features, improve things, and make the adjustments that are needed.

Lots of Resources if You Get Stuck

Because of all the benefits that come with Python, there are a lot of people who use this coding language. Some have this has their one and only resource to writing out codes, and some have it as part of their portfolio. Regardless of how people decide to use it, there are a ton of computer programmers who use and enjoy this language. As a result, there are a lot of resources available to you.

As a beginner, it is a great idea to take advantage of these resources as much as possible. If you need some help with doing a specific code, or you want to learn how to do something a little bitter, then you will need to head to the resources and see what they can do to help you out.

Doesn't Cost for You to Get Started

Another benefit of this language is that it won't cost you anything to get started. Computers and technology are expensive enough. If you are planning on getting really serious about your coding skills and some of the things that you can do with it, you may have already spent some money on the ability to do this. The fact that you can get the library with Python, the interpreter, and everything else that you need for free, makes this a great option for those who just want a chance to experiment and see how things go.

Since Python is an open sourced language, you get the benefit of working with a code that isn't going to cost anything. You will find that people can come in and use the code for any project that they want, and it is even possible for them to make changes and adjustments to the code, without having to pay for anything at all. These innovations are what keeps the language growing over time, and can make it easier for you to use the language for free as well.

Now, there are some components that you can purchase with this language if you choose. The basics that you need for writing code will be free. But if you would like to have a special interpreter or compiler to make things easier, or you want a special library that only one company makes, then you will need to purchase those. But you can get everything that you need in order to write your code for free if you don't want any of that extra stuff.

Improves Your Computer Skills Without Being Impossible to Learn

It doesn't matter if this is your very first programming language or you have learned one or two along the way. Learning Python can really help you to enhance your computer skills and can make you more marketable than every program before. IT jobs are opening everywhere, and even if you just want to create your own programs or work on the side, rather than taking this full time, learning Python can be the best option to help with this.

Python can enhance almost any kind of programing language as well. That is another benefit that comes with Python; it has the skills and the power to work with many other languages to get the work done right. You can choose how you want to use the language, too.

Do you have an idea for creating your own app or game but don't have the time or the patience to learn some of the more complicated languages? Would you like to start a part time career, making some money on the side, doing various programming activities? Python is the perfect option to go with if any of these sound like something you are dealing with.

However, just like any other programming languages, Python has its own limitations. For instance, it lacks some built-in features that are dominant in other modern programming languages. Therefore, it is important that you make use of Python modules, libraries, and frameworks to hasten custom software development. In accordance with several studies, we have also seen that Python is slower than some commonly used programming languages such as Java and C++.

You, therefore, have to fast-track the Python application by having some alterations in the application code or by use of customized runtime. Nevertheless, you can constantly use Python to accelerate software development and streamline software maintenance.

Chapter 13: Conditionals and Booleans

Earlier on, we talked about comparison operators and how they could be used to determine whether a statement within a language was true or false. This is where we get into one of the biggest concepts underlying any given program. If things were such that you always knew one thing or another, the world would be a very different place. However, this really isn't the case, and there are times where you have to evaluate a situation, make a determination, and then make a decision regarding that condition.

These kinds of situations are often very serious and demand your utmost response. For example, if your friend Rolf, who doesn't understand basic apple arithmetic, were trying to log into your computer, you would want it to tell him to go away. So how would we go about this? (We're going to use our first command to accept user input in this script, so saddle in for that as well.)

Create a new script. Call it what you like - I'll be calling mine login.py.

We want to create a few variables called username and password. Set username and password to anything that you want.

Ask the user to enter their username, like so:

userInput = raw_input("What is your username? ")

Now we're going to work some magic and have Python decide whether they entered the described username or not.

if userInput == username:

userInput = raw_input("Password? ")

else:

print "You entered the incorrect username."

We're going to get to the else part in a second, but for now, just save this and try to run it. Test it by entering the wrong username first, then run the program again and enter the correct username. If all goes well, you'll see the proper responses.

Now let's talk about what's happening here.

This is called an if/else statement, and is the most basic form of conditional decision making within Python (and most programming languages, for that matter.)

What happens is that you give it a statement that it evaluates the truthfulness of a given statement and then takes action based off of whether or not the statement was true.

What is occurring in that chunk of code up there is that it's evaluating whether or not userInput --
which is the string that we just had the user enter -- is the same as "username". If it is, then it
prompts the user for their password. If it isn't, then it tells them that they entered the wrong
username. Simple enough, right?

But we do have that personal vendetta against Mr. Rolf, so we should probably include that
within our code. But how? I mean, we've already got a completed if statement, right?

Wrong! There's another thing we can do, called an else if. Check this out:

```
if userInput == username:
userInput = raw_input("Password? ")
elif userInput == "rolf" or userInput == "Rolf" or userInput == "ROLF":
print "There is no room on this computer for Rolf."
else:
print "You have entered the incorrect username."
```

This evaluates the userInput to see if the username is "Rolf" or any variant thereof. String
comparison is innately case-sensitive, so "ROlf" would not be equal to "ROLf". How can we fix
this?

Well, we can simultaneously fix the case-sensitivity issue and make the code more elegant by
changing our else-if line to the following.

```
elif userInput.lower() == "rolf":
```

This converts whatever the userInput variable is to lowercase. We can now simply compare it to
lowercase "rolf" and the issue would be fixed.

You may have noticed the little **"or"**, and it might have caught you off guard. That's called a
boolean operator.

There are three primary boolean operators in Python: and, or, and not.

"And" is used to check two conditions and see if they both return true. If either returns false, then
the whole thing returns false. So to use the apple values from the last script, if we were to write
this:

```
if myApples == 5 and friendApples == 6:
```

It'd come back as true. However, if even **one** of those weren't true, the whole thing would return
false.

"Or" is similar, but it checks to see if **either** condition or expression is true. If even one is true, the whole thing comes back true.

"Not" checks to see if a boolean/condition/expression is **not** true. For the sake of illustration and exposition, you can actually put a single boolean variable into an if-statement, because an if statement only checks to see if whatever following it is true.

If you had a variable called "IAmCool" which is set to True, and you typed:

if IAmCool:

print "I am cool"

It would actually print "I am cool", because the if-statement sees that as a true statement. Following?

Now, if IAmCool were set to False because the only thing stronger than your self-deprecating sense of humor is your will to teach yourself various programming languages, and you instead of "if IAmCool" typed this:

if not IAmCool:

print "I am not cool"

It would check to see if IAmCool were **false**.

So between if, else if, and else statements, you've got a pretty solid chunk of conditional decision making under wraps.

Let's go back to that code we had just a moment ago.

if userInput == username:

userInput = raw_input("Password? ")

elif userInput.lower() == "rolf":

print "There is no room on this computer for Rolf."

else:

print "You have entered the incorrect username."

We got the username, and it was right. Where do we go from here?

This is where we start to utilize a concept known as **nested conditional statements**. You can put an if-statement within an if-statement!

This is your time to shine, friend. After prompting for the password, write another if-statement **within** that if-statement, as well as an else statement. You need to compare userInput to your variable password and see if they're the same. If they are, you need to welcome the user; if they aren't, you need to tell them that they've entered the wrong password.

By the end, your code should look like this:

```
if userInput == username:
    userInput = raw_input("Password? ")
    if userInput == password:
        print "Welcome!"
    else:
        print "That's the wrong password."
elif [...]
```

If it does, then you succeeded.

Chapter 14: Lists and Loops

Lists in Python are very straightforward.

Let's say that we wanted to create a list of our favorite TV shows. We could do this like so:

favoriteShows = ['Breaking Bad', 'Narcos', 'House of Cards']

These are all different elements in a list which starts counting at 0. You can also access the lists rather simply.

If you were to type the following:

print favoriteShows[0]

Then it would print out the first element of the list, here being Breaking Bad.

You can also enter data into a list rather simply! Lists have a built in function called "append()" which allows you to add data to the list, like so:

listExample.append(raw_input())

This would take the user's input and add it to the function. (It's also an example of calling a function as an argument of a function, which makes no sense at all right now but hopefully will in the next chapter!)

You can actually declare empty lists to be used, as well. You'd do so by declaring the variable and setting it with empty brackets, like this:

emptyList = []

From here, you could add elements to the list and start to use it like you would any other list.

To move to the next portion of the lesson and get off the whole list tangent, we should talk about loops. Loops are an integral part of many programs. They serve a great many purposes, but at their most basic level they're simply a way for a chunk of code within a program to repeat multiple times, most likely changing in one way or another each time.

There are three main kinds of loops in Python: while, for, and do...while. All of these have their own particular uses that they're tailored for.

While loops are the simplest, they execute over and over for as long as a given condition still comes back as true, and that's all there really is to it.

Observe the following code:

```
dogs = 0
while (dogs <= 10):
print "There are %d dogs in the yard!"
dogs += 1


print "Wow! That's a lot of dogs!"
```

Can you guess what's happening here? We declared a variable called dogs and we set it to 0. We then started the while loop, giving it a condition. **While** the variable dogs is less than or equal to 10, we want to run this loop. Every iteration of this loop will print "There are **x** dogs in the yard!", and the loop increments every single time.

For loops are similar to while loops, but they automatically increment over a set of data, such as the lists we were talking about earlier.

You don't necessarily have to iterate over lists. Python has a built-in range function that lets you iterate through a certain number of variables. For example, a for loop iterating through range(5) would iterate 5 times, from 0 to 4. Let's use this to count to 5.

Here's an example of that for loop:

```
for i in range(5):
print "%d" % (i + 1)
```

Simple enough, right? Not too hard at all. We can also iterate through lists like earlier. If we wanted to print out every TV show on our list from earlier, we could do something like: print "My favorite shows are: "

```
for i in favoriteShows:
print "%s" % i
```

The i is what's called a loop variable, and in Python, it assumes the type of whatever your list is made of. Since lists can hold mixed values (even at once), this is great and super important.

Let's actually start working with this and combining a lot of the concepts that we've worked on. Create a new file, call it what you like but I'm going to call mine bookList.py.

The first thing that we're going to do is create an empty list of books and a boolean called running set to True.

```
bookList                                    =                          []
running = True
```

Now what we're going to do is create something called a running loop. This is to show you a way that while loops can be used.

We're going to create a loop that runs for as long as the variable "running" is true.

```
while running == True:
```

The first thing we're going to do within the loop is prompt the user to add a book, list the current books, or exit the program. We're going to want to compare the response to other things, so we need to set it to a variable.

```
userInput = raw_input("Book List v1.\nType \"add\" to add a book, \"list\" to list the books, or \"exit\" to exit the program: ")
```

Now we need to parse the input and compare it. First, we're going to see if the user wanted to add a book, and add a book if they did:

```
if                     userInput.lower()              ==                "add":
userInput       =      raw_input("Enter      the      name      of      the      book:      \n")
bookList.append(userInput)
```

Perfect. There's actually a way to simplify that line by just passing the function "raw_input('...')" to bookList.append, but I wanted to show you that you can append any variable to your list.

Now we're going to determine what happens if the user entered "list", which should be checking to see if the list is empty and printing out its contents if not:

```
elif                     userInput.lower()              ==                "list":
if   not   bookList:   #   this   is   shorthand   for   "if   the   bookList   is   empty"
print                "The              list              is              empty!\n"
else:
for                     i                     in                     bookList:
print "%s\n" % i # prints everything on the list
```

Now, if the user entered "exit", we need to set the variable running to false so that we exit the main loop, since it's only supposed to run while the variable running is true.

```
elif                     userInput.lower()              ==                "exit":
running = False
```

And lastly, if they entered anything **but** "add", "list", or "exit", we need to print that their command was invalid.

```
else:
print "The command was invalid!\n"
```

This is the first major program we've done so far, but this is a very cursory introduction to variables, loops, and input/output.

From here on out, we're going to be introducing concepts by working on this specific file, so you need to hold this file near and dear.

Chapter 15: Functions

Functions are an integral part of any given programming language. They supply a way to define something that's supposed to happen and may have to happen many times or basic functions of the program in general, and reuse that chunk of code as often as you need to. They also allow you to modify existing values and work with variables that you already have.

The basic breakdown of a function in pseudocode is like this:

function(parameter1, parameter2, **etc...) {**
do things
}
And it will normally be called within your main portion of code or from other functions like so:
function(variable1, variable2**)**

Functions can be used to massively simplify abrasively verbose code and make it much easier to understand, while at the same time making it more modular and reusable.

So how do you work with functions in Python? They follow a very simple structure.

In order to declare a function in Python, you simply type:

def functionName(arguments)**:** code here

That's really all that there is to it. The parameters that you define for a function can be used within the body of that function's code. When you call the function later on, you can put any values of the same type in the place. The best way to explain it is that the parameters you use in your function definition are **hypothetical**, and are intended to be replaced with actual values.

If we wanted to code a function which was to take the length and width of a rectangle, find the area, and return that value, we could do it like this:

```
def findArea(length, width):
return length * width
```

You could then call this later in your code. You can use actual values, like so:

```
area = findArea(4, 6) # "area" would have the value of 24
```

Or you can use already existent variables in order to call the function.

```
l = 6
w = 3
area = findArea(l, w) # "area" would have the value of 18
```

You can even use other functions as arguments, since every function simply returns a value.

```
def add(number1, number2):
return number1 + number2

def findArea(length, width):
return length * width

area = findArea(4, add(2,2))
```

This code would first do the add function which would return the value 4, then multiply the return value of the add function by the first argument (4). It would ultimately return the value of 16.

So the question now is, how can we use functions in order to pretty up our existing code and make it more functional? Let's go back to our bookList code. It's perfectly functional, right? But looking at it is a mess. Let's give functions to our addBook and listBook functions, and make them a little bit more, well, functional while we're at it.

So let's look at the if statement for adding a book.

```
if userInput.lower() == "add":
userInput = raw_input("Enter the name of the book.\n"
bookList.append(userInput)
```

What we want to do is make this so it's simpler, like so:

```
if userInput.lower90 == "add":
addBook(bookList)
```

Here's how we'd do this. Functions have to be declared and defined before you call them. You can do it anywhere before. I'm going to do it at the beginning right after our variableList.

```
def addBook(bList):
userInput = raw_input("Enter the name of the book you'd like to add.\n")
bList.append(userInput)
```

You could have named the variable **bList** anything, even **bookList** - the reason I didn't name it bookList for simplicity's sake is in order to drive home the point that function parameters are only hypothetical values that you replace with real values when you call them.

Now if we replace our current if-statement with this:

```
if userInput.lower() == "add":
addBook(bookList)
```

It should work perfectly fine.

Now we need to add a function which will allow us to list the books. This is going to be much the same: we need to send it our list, bookList, and have it read it off. First we need to define it. I'm putting it right after our last function:

```
def listBooks(listOfBooks):
```

Now we need to transfer our logic over.

```
def listBooks(listOfBooks):
if not listOfBooks:
print "The list is empty!\n"
else:
for i in listOfBooks:
print "%s\n" % i
```

After that, we can go back to our if-statement and replace the ugly code with the far more elegant:

```
elif userInput.lower() == "list":
listBooks(bookList)
```

Save and run your code to ensure that it works. It should go just fine. By the end, it should look a bit like this:

```
bookList = []
running = True

def addBook(bList):
userInput = raw_input("Enter the name of the book you'd like to add.\n")
bList.append(userInput)

def listBooks(listOfBooks):
if not listOfBooks:
print "The list is empty!\n"
```

```
else:
    for i in listOfBooks:
        print "%s\n" % i


while running == True:
    userInput = raw_input("Book List v1.\nType \"add\" to add a book, \"list\" to list the books, or \"exit\" to exit\n") if userInput.lower() == "add":
        addBook(bookList)
    elif userInput.lower() == "list":
        listBooks(bookList)
    elif userInput.lower() == "exit":
        running = False
    else:
        print "The command was invalid!\n"
```

Notice how much cleaner and easier to read that our primary code is, starting at the run loop and going to the end of the program.

Chapter 16: Basic Object-Oriented Programming: Objects and Classes

Python is an object-oriented programming language. In fact, most modern languages are. But what exactly does this mean? We've spoken in vague terms of objects and classes but we haven't really established quite what this actually means in in any certain terms one way or another.

An object is an instance of a class. Most things you'll deal with in Python are objects. Earlier, when we worked with file input and output, we created instances of a file class.

A class is a way of defining objects. This sounds terribly vague, but let's look at it this way.

You likely have or have had a pet, right? Let's say there's a dog, and his name is Roscoe.

Well, Roscoe is an animal. Animals have broad, generally defined characteristics, but they're all animals, much like Roscoe is an animal. Get comfy with Roscoe, because we're going to be talking him a lot while we talk about the relations between classes and the relations between classes and objects.

We've established that Roscoe is **most certainly** an animal. He fits the definition of an animal. In this manner, Roscoe is a specific instance of the animal class. If you were writing a simulation of life, and you had people and animals, you would define Roscoe as an instance of **animal**, just as you declared variable **file1** as an instance of **file**, or you declared **tonguetwister** as an instance of **string**.

Now, we need to talk about how we actually define a class and an object within Python.

Create a new file to work with, I'm calling mine pursuitOfRoscoe.py.

Within this file, we're going to start right out the bat by defining a class.

To declare a class, you follow the following template:

class **name**(parent)

We're on our way to defining Roscoe, now. We need a way to define an animal. Let's think about what most animals have. Most animals have legs, that's a start. Animals also have Latin names. Let's work with those two. If your class stores data, you generally need to have an initializer function within your class.

Perfect. Since Roscoe's a dog, he'll have 4 legs, and his species is Canis Lupus Familiaris.

With that in mind, we now have a definition for animal classes that can be used amongst many animals, not just Roscoe. That's the entire idea behind classes: creating reusable data structures for any given object so that the code is more readable, easy to understand, cleaner, and portable, among other buzzword adjectives that are surprisingly very, very true.

How do we declare an instance of this class now? Like anything else!

roscoe = Animal(4, "Canis Lupus Familiaris")

We can go in and change these variables too. Canis lupus is so formal, and Roscoe's our buddy, so let's change that to Roscoe.

roscoe.name = "Roscoe"

There we go. **Much** better.

Hopefully, this makes the distinction between classes and objects **much** clearer.

Roscoe is a dog, and an animal. Thus he takes from the common concept of being an animal. Since he's an instance of an animal, he automatically receives the traits that all animals have. How cool is that?

Let's go a bit further, and incorporate some functions. What's something that every animal does? Sleep. Every single animal sleeps, aside from Ozzy Osborne.

Let's give animals a function so that they can sleep.

Below our initializer, create a new function called sleep that takes the arguments of **self** and **hours**. Then print out a line of text that says the animal's name and how long it's sleeping for. My code ended up looking a bit like this, and hopefully yours will as well.

```
def sleep(self, hours):
print "%s is sleeping for %d hours!" % (self.name, hours)
```

Then below our declaration of Roscoe, let's go ahead and run the "sleep" function with the argument of 4 hours.

```
roscoe = Animal(4, "canis lupus familiaris")
roscoe.name = "Roscoe"
roscoe.sleep(4)
```

Save this and run it. If all goes well, it should print out "Roscoe is sleeping for 4 hours!".

To start is the objects. These objects are going to be anything that can match up with things in the real world. They could be things like a ball, a car, food, or anything else that would be an object in the real world, outside of the programming language. You will find that there are a ton of objects inside the coding language of Python, and you can create an object for any of the different parts of the code that you would like.

Classes can be a great way to organize all of these different objects. Inside the code, you don't want the different objects to just float around on their own. This can make things a mess and will get things lost. The compiler won't know what to bring out when you use a command for it, and you are going to run into a lot of problems because of this. In fact, if you don't spend some time setting up the classes that you want to work with, it is likely that you are going to get a lot of error messages in the code, and you will have no idea how to fix the problem.

You can make as many classes as you would like, and they can be related to any subject or topic that you would like. When you create a class, it is like creating an empty box that you plan to fill up as you work on the code. You can fill up the box with anything that you would like. You just need to make sure that all the objects that are in the same class have some kind of relationship to each other, and that it makes sense that they end up in the same class together.

This doesn't mean that all the objects need to be the same as each other. You can have some different things in there, but you need to have it set up so that someone who looks at the class understands why certain objects are placed in that same class together.

So, when you create a class, you may decide to put one together that is about food. This means that everything that would go in that class would have to be some kind of food. You can pick a combination of fruits, vegetables, meats, dairy, sweets, and more. As long as they are a type of food, then they fit into the class.

But if you set up a class that is for blue vehicles, this doesn't mean that you can throw in any old vehicle that you would like. You can put a blue van, a blue car, a blue truck, and a blue motorcycle inside. But if you have a red car, it shouldn't be added to the class and you will have to either leave it out or choose a different kind of class to add it to.

As you can see, working with these classes can be relatively easy to do. They do a great job at keeping you organized and makes it easier for the compiler to complete the commands that you send over to it. Let's spend some more time looking at some more about these classes and objects and how to use them to enhance your code.

What are the Objects and Classes in Python?

Python is a programming language oriented around objects. The term object in this definition refers to the object you already know – something tangible, you can label, feel, sense, and manipulate. When it comes to software development, an object may not be tangible but it is still a model of something that can be labeled and manipulated.

Simply put, an object in object-oriented programming is a collection of labeled data as well as its associated behaviors. They include variables (data) and associated methods (functions) that act on those variables. A class may be defined as a template that has all the details about an object.

Creating class in python

Now that we are familiar with the syntax for creating a class in Python, we'll introduce a class example called Dog.

class Dog:

"Dog class"

    var1 = "Bark"

    var2 = "Jump"

In Python 3, there is no difference between class declaration and class definition. This is because the two occur simultaneously. Class definition follows declaration and documentation string as demonstrated in our example.

Chapter 17: How Do You Write a Good Code?

The next thing that we need to take a look at is how to write out a good code. The way that we are going to do this, to make things easier, is to write out your first example of a code in Python. This is going to just a line long, but it will have some of the basic components that you read about above and is a good place to start. We are looking to see how the compiler will read through the information that you set up, how you can make the code work, and all the other steps that you need.

Before you are able to do much with Python and making it work for your own codes, it is important to know the basics of writing a code.

The first thing that you need to do is open up your text editor. The text editor gives you a fast way to create and test out programs to gain some familiarity with the basics of doing this. It can help you to create your programs, save them so you can use them later on, and teach you how to run those newly created programs through your interpreter. This will also help you test out whether you installed the interpreter in the proper manner.

Once the text editor is open, you will be creating a print statement. When you work in Python, print will be one of the keywords you work with frequently, and it is considered one of the basic functions that come with this language. The print command is often going to be used to help display the right information inside the terminal during the program.

At this point, you want to add in your statement. In order to easily test out what you know about a programming language, use the "Hello, World!" idea. You can add this text inside your print() statement part, and make sure that there are some quotation marks around the statement that you want to show off. So, to start with the hello world program, you would type out

print("Hello, World!");

Unlike what you can find with a lot of the other coding languages, you will indicate where a line ends using a ";". Additionally, you can avoid the curly braces to designate blocks. Usually doing an indent is enough to make this work for your coding needs.

After you have written out the code that we have above, it is time to save that file. You can click on the File menu that is found in your text editor, and make sure that you select Save As. Navigate to the drop-down menu below the name box, select the type of file in Python that you would like to use. If you happen to be using Notepad, which is not recommended, you would select All Files, and ensure that ".py" is visible at the end of the file name.

When you are saving, make sure that you save the file in an easily accessible location. Later, take the time to work your way through the command prompt to find the information later on, and if you make it too difficult to find, this can end up being a pain. For this file, you may want to consider calling it something like "hello.py:

Now it is time to actually run the program that you just wrote. You can open up the Command Prompt or the Terminal and then find your way back to where the file was saved. When you find the right location, you can run the file by simply typing in hello.py.m then, press on the Enter button. If you did all the other steps properly, you will see the words "Hello, World!" show up on your screen below the command prompt.

Depending on the method that you used to install Python, and which version you are operating with, it may be necessary to type python hello.py or python3 hello.py instead in order for the program to run.

When you are writing out your own codes, make sure that you stop and test them out as often as possible. The nice thing about working in the Python language is that you get the ability to test out all of your new programs right away. A good way to do this is to make sure that the command prompt and the editor opened at the same time. By saving the updates directly in your editor, you are able to run the program from your command line immediately. If changes are needed, you can go back and make them in the editor before testing again.

Testing is sometimes seen as a waste of time, but it can really help to avoid a lot of problems along the way. If you insist upon going through and writing out the whole code without testing it once and then an error message comes up, how are you going to have any idea on what is causing that error message and what you need to work on fixing to make it go away?

If you only write out a few lines of code at a time before testing, you can easily tell where the mistakes happen when they start showing up on the screen. You can do a line or two, check it out, and then easily figure out where the mistake is when an error comes up. It is much easier to do it in this manner rather than trying to go through a whole program worth of code to find the different errors.

Examples of Coding

Loops

Loops are generally utilized whenever one computer system is used when there is a program needed to repeat processes more than once. This particular process is referred to as 'iteration' and there will end up being 1 loop that is 'for' and the other is called a 'while' loop in Python. The first image is a representation of the 'for' loop and the 2nd image is the easiest of the two and is the 'while' loop.

Working with Numbers

Develop your machine code process to develop zeros direct into computer memory. The start address is given at address 0x80 and the number of words to develop is given at address 0x84. We assume the start address is word aligned and the number of words to develop is greater than zero.

Working with Strings

Strings as part of python, frequently tend to be a conterminous collection of recognizable possibility delimited through a line or possibly multiple quotes. Python wouldn't possess any kind of distinct information range for a recognizable possibility; therefore, they frequently tend to be portrayed as the lone recognizable string.

Creating strings

It is essentially the string of recognizable possibility; the string takes place to be as part of the fact. The recognizable takes place to be as part of the character. For example, the English language has 26 recognizable possibilities.

Computer systems do not contend with mere possibility. They contend with actual numbers (with decimal points included). It is quite possibly an option, however, that you may not notice any recognizable options on your display screen inside. It takes place to be as part of the fact actually store and analyzed as a series and combinations of zeros (o) and ones (1).

This conversion process recognizable to the number takes place to be a part of fact called encoding. The reverse process takes place to be as part of the fact called decoding. ASCII and Unicode frequently tend to be more of the favored among users and especially beginners, as it relates to Python strings, which tend to take place in a hidden bit of Unicode that remains recognizable.

Unicode was originally coded to include all things considered and bring consistency as a major aspect of encoding. You can take in additional about Unicode from here.

Strings as a Python Feature:

Strings can be made through encasing unmistakable probability inside singular quotation marks or multiple quotes. It is up to you what your desired outcome will be. For the most part, Python is typically used to be a representation of multiple strings and doc-strings.

When you run the program, your specific output will be: If ran and executed properly.

There are numerous tasks that can be performed with the string that makes it a standout amongst the most utilized types of data in Python.

Link of Two or More Strings - Joining of at least two strings into a solitary one is called "concatenation".

The "+" function allows you to compose 2 string literals together and links them.

The " *" function can be utilized to rehash the string for a set number of repetitions.

Chapter 18: The MySQL Database: Create and Use the Database

Many computer programs, including content management systems, photo galleries, and blogs, will need to have some system in place to help them store and then retrieve data. For example, when you work on a blog, you will need some place where you can store your posts, and then have it so that a visitor can read them on your site. When it comes to a photo gallery, you need to have a place that is able to store information about the pictures and can bring them back out each time that you want to see a specific picture that you stored.

Instead of coming up with a different piece of software, or a different database to handle this each time, all of these are going to use specialized database programs that can be modified to fit their needs. To make it easier for other programs to access data through them, it is common for database software to support SQL, which is a type of computer language that works well just for databases.

There are a lot of different databases that are going to support this SQL to access their data. And one of these is going to be MySQL. MySQL is just a brand of one database software, of which there are many that you can work with. This is a very popular one to use with websites, often because it is free, and you will see them advertised on many of the sites that you visit.

MySQL is an Oracle-based open source relational database management system. It has the ability to work on almost all platforms, including Windows, UNIX, and Linux. Although there are a lot of different applications that can be used with this, it is often associated with things related to online publishing and web applications. Many of the top websites that you may visit, as well as consumer and corporate facing web-based applications will use this database system. This includes some popular sites like YouTube, Twitter, and Facebook.

MySQL is going to be a client-server model. The server of this is able to handle all of the commands, or the database instructions, that it is given. It is available in two formats. The first is as a separate program to be used in a client-server networked environment. The second is as a library that is able to be linked or embedded into different applications.

Originally, this service was developed in order to handle large databases in a quick manner. While this software is going to just be installed on one main machine, it can send that database to many different locations. And any user that wants to can access it through the various interfaces that are available. These interfaces are able to send out SQL statements to the server and when it is time display the results.

The MySQL is going to enable data to be stored and accessed through many storage engines, such as NBD,CVS<, and InnoDB. It also able to replicate data and partition tables for better performance and durability. System users are not going to have to learn new commands because they can just use the standard commands that they learned when working with SQL.

MySQL is written out in C++ and C, and are able to be accessed through more than 20 different platforms, though most commonly found in Mac, Windows, Linux, and Unix. The RDBMS is going to be able to support a very large database with millions of records and make it simple to discover information that you really need - within seconds.

The main difference that you are going to see between SQL and MySQL before 2016, was that the latter is going to be used on a variety of platforms, while the other one was only available on Windows. In 2017, though, Microsoft expanded SQL to operate with Linux. When you are installing SQL using Linux, the package management system will ask the user to do some custom configuration in order to optimize how it works and to provide the right amount of security for the system.

In addition, MySQL has the advantage of allowing users to select the most efficient storage engine for any given table because the program can use several storage engines to deal with an individual table. One of the engines that comes with this is the InnoDB. InnoDB was engineered for high availability. But that means it isn't always as fast as some of the other engines. Still, it provides you with a lot of the benefits that you are looking for.

On the other hand, SQL will use a storage system of its own, but it does help add in some different safeguards to protect against any loss of data. You will see that both of these systems will run in clusters to help with high availability.

You will also find that SQL Server is a choice that you can make that offers a lot of reporting tools and data analysis tools. SQL Server Reporting Services is very popular and available to download for free. There are also some other reporting tools that you can choose to download and use along with this program if they work for you.

Conclusion

Thank you for making it through to the end of the book. Running Python on a computer has proven to be a success. As a beginner in Python, it is key to keep your mind wide open for new encounters. The above, are the steps required to ensure that your computer is running python smoothly.

Remain focused, as you are on this journey to learning programming. You will not become great overnight. It is always a great thing to see a programmer turn into a millionaire or a programmer changing the lives of thousands in a single programming day.

Ultimately this book was written with the goal in mind of teaching you not necessarily about Python, but programming at large.

If you are reading this, it means that you have made it to the end of the book. One word for you?

When you make a clear and realistic plan of how you aim to learn, the plan becomes achievable. Learning will definitely be at your own pace. The first step is the interest that you had, which resulted in you reading this book and then – action! Challenge yourself with new tasks every day. Programming is not as hard as it looks or as hard as people make it seem. Nothing is hard if you are ready to put in the work. Start with the basics.

Most of the people who are new to programming and who want to learn use Python. Even though most programmers say it is an easy program to learn, it will all depend on you. If you are to have a chance at being successful in this, you will need to go the extra mile. Ask questions from experts and always be ready and eager to learn. Who knows? This could be a step in learning all the programming languages out there. Keep an open mind and you will not find anything hard about this.

The next step is to use this knowledge to your advantage. Do something with it. You can absolutely use this book as a reference, but it wasn't written to necessarily be one - this book was written in order to teach you the essence of programming and everything that you need to do to start programming in Python, as well as the essential tools of the language that you'll have to know how to use as a beginner.

www.ingramcontent.com/pod-product-compliance
Lightning Source LLC
Chambersburg PA
CBHW031246050326
40690CB00007B/981